Jennie's Bo Jangles

JENNIE'S BO JANGLES

Joyce Elizabeth Wagley

VANTAGE PRESS
New York / Washington / Atlanta
Los Angeles / Chicago

FIRST EDITION

Copyright © 1986 by Joyce Elizabeth Wagley

Published by Vantage Press, Inc.
516 West 34th Street, New York, New York 10001

Manufactured in the United States of America
ISBN: 0-533-06936-X

Library of Congress Catalog Card No.: 85-91426

A tribute to Bob

Jennie's Bo Jangles

Chapter One

It was a rainy May morning when Jennie first foaled. It had been a long eleven months of waiting. The last ten days had been particularly anxious. Jennie had watched her pasture-mate, Carmen, produce a strong colt, and focus all her attention on him. Jennie was kept at bay.

Jennie was ten years old but had never foaled before. Would she have any problems? How would she adapt to being a dam?

Larry took the phone call at the seminary, where he was a professor, from the farm's neighbor who checked the horses daily.

"The gray mare's foaled. You've got another black one. It looks okay." George's message had been short.

When Larry phoned Joyce with the news, she asked, "What is it?"

"He didn't say. The conversation was short."

"Oh, I'm so excited. How can I work all day?"

"Relax, Jennie's fine. I've called the vet. He will go to the farm after 5 o'clock. I'll drive by home after I leave the seminary to see if you're there. If not, I'll meet you at the farm. Oh, yes, congratulations!"

By noon, Joyce declared she couldn't keep her mind on work a minute longer, made arrangements for her classes to be taken care of, and left to drive to "The Back 40." She stopped at home long enough to change into old clothes and rain boots. Grabbing the camera and a package of carrots, she was on her way.

It was a long, forty-five minute drive. The rain had slackened to a fine mist, with the sun peeking out from gray clouds, by the time Joyce reached the outer gate. Everything smelled fresh and the birds were singing. As always, she felt renewed with the peace of the place.

Nearing the inside gate, Joyce could see Jennie and Carmen looking over as if they'd been waiting. Quickly, she hopped out of the car, walking slowly and talking to the mares in a soft voice. "Okay now, it's all right. I've come to see Jennie's surprise. That's a good mama."

Carmen's colt, Magic, popped his head through the gate slats. Where was the new foal? Then, as she reached the gate, she saw a little black body standing by Jennie. *Oh, it's so tiny and wet.*

Slipping through the gate, Joyce patted Carmen and gave her a large hunk of carrot. Then, to Jennie, with the rest of the carrot. As she peered around Jennie to get a closer look—poof!—the little black shape disappeared. What happened? Then she spotted two little black legs, now on the other side of Jennie. She moved back to look, only to watch the foal disappear again. It had simply moved under his dam to be on the other side. Joyce watched this procedure several more times and noted the foal cleared Jennie easily.

Jennie looked fine—possibly a little drawn. It was obvious she was proud and protective of her prize.

"Ah, Jennie, it's darling, so little—except for the ears and knobby knees. But is it a colt or a filly?"

Jennie turned to nozzle the foal, who was beginning to nurse, as if to say, "What does it matter?" Joyce had not been raised on a farm like Larry. But she had thought she could figure that mystery out.

"I think you're a colt, but I'm not sure." How embarrassing if the vet asked her before he saw the foal.

Joyce was entranced, as she watched the little black one move around and under his mama on the little wobbly legs. He tended to stand parallel with her. If she moved, so did he.

"Well, if you are a little colt, your name is Jennie's Bo. How's that? Your papa's name is Bo. I wonder if he was ever this tiny?"

Jennie and Bo Jangles (one day old)

It began to rain a little harder. "Let's get to the barn. I know you mares are hungry."

Carmen led, with Magic trotting along. Jennie followed, with the little foal having to move fast to keep up. But he stayed in shadow position.

The mares were eager, as always, for the grain. The foals suckled their snack and then, being both full and warm in the dry barn, plopped down by the mares on the straw.

"You can stay in the barn for a while to rest. Jennie, I'm so proud of you." Joyce stroked the contented mare as she gazed fondly at her little sleeping foal.

Larry arrived before the vet. He was happy, but not as excited as he'd been on the Sunday morning he'd found Magic.

"But what is it?" Joyce asked.

"I'm not sure. A colt, I think, but it's hard to tell."

Even the vet didn't say after his first appraisal. He reached down, picked up the foal by its tiny hooves, and let it land on its back.

"Umph." The slightly dazed foal stood up again, and his little stallion parts were visible.

"Then you are Jennie's Bo—Little Bo." More interested in nursing than in his naming, the little colt happily suckled away.

"Well, you have two fine colts, and the mares are doing well." The vet declined coffee this time and left the barn to go out into the rain. He could be heard speaking to his office on the two-way radio, to find out if there were more stops to make before heading home for supper.

Because of the rain, Jennie and Little Bo spent the night in the barn, even though Jennie voiced her objection. Both the mares thought a barn was fine to eat in, but they liked the freedom to return to the pasture.

The next three days were rainy. Joyce and Larry drove back and forth from the city each day to feed the mares and check the new colts.

Then it was the weekend and there was more time for watching and stroking the colts, picture-taking, and catching up on chores. Friends came to get acquainted with Little Bo and to take more pictures. Always the little colt shadowed his mama and disappeared under her if he felt threatened. Jennie was relaxing more and grazing contentedly.

Sunday morning, after feeding the mares and watching the colts, Joyce and Larry had a leisurely breakfast on the deck.

Joyce sipped her coffee. "I can't recall having been this happy and pleased with life in a long time. What a pretty spring this is."

"It's been raining a lot."

"Yes, but you know what I mean. Even with the rain, look how beautiful it is."

"I know. It's always nice here. And having those two little colts in the pasture is even more fun than I imagined it would be."

"Carmen's Secret Magic and Jennie's Bo. How does that sound?"

"I'll call mine Bo's Secret Magic, and how about Jennie's Bo Jangles?"

"Oh, I like that. It seems to fit. But I'll call him Little Bo for a while."

"He is small—but he's her first," Larry commented as he got up from his chair. "I'm going up to work on the fence in the front pasture. See you later." He caressed her shoulder as he passed.

"Fine." Joyce cleared the breakfast dishes and carried them in to the kitchen sink. Then, returning to the deck with her mug of coffee, she sat in a chair and looked over the wooded valley below. The sun was shining through the leafing trees, giving the valley an almost ethereal look. Various yellow and lilac wild flowers scattered down the rocky bluff. The thin clouds were clearing to a pale blue sky. Two woodpeckers were busy on an old dead tree, and the squirrels were chasing each other through the treetops, occasionally stopping to scold.

What a difference this place has made, thought Joyce. *And who would have ever thought I would fall in love with an old gray mare.*

Chapter Two

The decision to buy this forty acres had been made quickly four springs ago. One Sunday in April, Joyce and Larry had been sitting in their his and hers chairs, reading the Kansas City Star. She was looking at a book review in the arts section, and he was poring over the ads—a favorite pastime.

"Anything interesting?" Joyce idly asked.

"Uhmm—just looking at the farm ads."

The possibility of a rural retreat was a hopeful dream. Larry folded the paper into three columns and went to the phone.

"Well, you sounded pretty interested about something," Joyce remarked as Larry returned to the living room.

"Some of the prospects for farm acreage sounded pretty good. I think I'll check into some of them this week. Remember, no classes at St. Paul."

"Yes, I remember."

The next evening after work, Joyce was busily typing up a final term paper for her extension course when Larry came home.

"Hi—have a good day?" she asked, without looking up from her notes.

"Yes, I did, and I want to talk to you when you are free there."

Joyce studied him a moment and knew he was serious. "Okay, but I need to get this done. Dinner is in the oven, and I'll be all through here in about an hour. Then we'll have all evening to talk."

She busily pecked away, glad the paper was at the point of just being typed. She could do that mechanically. It would be hard to concentrate on the subject of humanism when she was so curious.

They talked for a long time over the dinner table. Larry was waiting for her after work the next day, and they drove south for about an hour until they reached some farmland.

"I never knew there was land like this in Kansas. It looks like some of the bluffs in southern Illinois. It's beautiful here in the spring."

"I think it could be nice here any season."

Joyce agreed. On the way home, they were already talking about "our farm."

The forty-acre land was purchased. In May, Larry had a road put in to the house-site they had selected about a quarter of a mile back from the country gravel road. He started building a barn up the hill.

"Why the barn?"

"Ahh, these will be stalls one, two, three, and four."

"Silly, we don't have horses."

"But we will! Anyway, I need a place to store materials. And I can catch water from the roof and store it in a cistern for our water supply."

"Clever boy." Joyce was caught up in Larry's long-range planning of possibilities.

Their son, Steve, came home from college. He had agreed to spend his summer helping build the house. It had always been a sort of dream for Larry and Steve that they could do this. And what better experience for an architectural student?

Much of the first month was spent digging a foundation on the rocky bluff. Steve hacked away with a pick-ax. His grandfather came to help set the same rocks and stones back into a foundation. Larry was at the site when he wasn't teaching. They had bought an old Datsun truck to haul materials from Kansas City.

Joyce was amazed, once the foundation was complete, how fast the house went up. Christina, their daughter from Denver, flew home to help the week the floor was laid. It felt good having the family working together on the project. They began talking about a name for the place

Miraculously, the house was built and it stood. Steve and a friend finished the roof the week before he headed back to the university in Utah. All that remained to winterize the house was to set in the sixteen glass panels across the front. Those were in by October.

The woods surrounding the house and down the bluff were beautiful during the midwest autumn. As they walked along the bluff and in the fields, Larry remarked, "It will really be neat riding the horses this time of year."

"What horses? Are you going to try to saddle up some of thoses mares in the next 160 acres?"

"No, our horses. Remember, the barn."

Ah, well, let him dream, thought Joyce. *I have a retreat house.*

Larry began working on the inside of the house whenever he had free time during the winter. Joyce was busy taking more graduate classes. Also, she was having physical problems. Her arthritis was flaring up in new and painful ways.

The next summer Steve was home only six weeks, but he and Larry managed to finish most of the inside work. Joyce was little help, as she struggled with persistent pain. She enjoyed sitting on the deck, but when Larry talked about horses, she thought riding would be about the last thing she could do.

Christina came for a visit, bringing a sign that officially named the place "The Back 40."

The house was completed. Then Larry and Joyce were into plans for a three-month sabbatical study in England. Shortly after their return, Christina planned to marry, so there was a wedding to get ready for. Only short trips to The Back 40 could be managed. Larry always found something else that needed to be done to the land or a fence. Joyce enjoyed any opportunity to retreat—usually reading or knitting on the deck or in by the fireplace. Another year went by.

"Come rest awhile on the deck. Another pretty spring to enjoy." She handed him a glass of iced tea.

"Well, there's always something to do. After a while he continued, "I was checking out the pasture. I think we'll have a pretty good stand of lespedeza this year. It will be good for grazing. I'm going to get a horse."

Chapter Three

Larry found his mare soon with the help of a colleague who owned and showed Missouri Fox Trotters. Bob bought the mare's yearling to enter the following year in the futurity for two-year-old Fox Trotters. Larry took the mare, Secret Carmen, to be bred with Bob's winning stallion, Bo's Black Magic.

Joyce went along to see the mare. She liked the black mare with the white blaze. Carmen had a gentle disposition.

"Now, we must find one for you," Larry said on the way home.

"Oh, I don't know. I'm not sure I could ride."

"Yes, you will. You're doing better. And a Fox Trotter's broken gait is a smooth ride. Besides, Carmen needs a pasture-mate.

"Well, see what you can find."

Larry learned of a gray mare for sale and urged Joyce to go with him to check her out. She agreed without much enthusiasm. On the way to the stables, they picked up a friend who told them about the mare.

"She's really a dear and has a nice broken gait. The owner just hasn't had time for her in several years. Once he showed her and won some ribbons. I'd like her myself, if I could afford another horse."

The gray mare was in a back pasture with other horses when they arrived. She responded to the attention and eagerly ate the carrot.

Larry looked at her intently. "Her hooves need trimming

and she needs a good brushing, but she's alert." He coaxed her to run a little, trying to watch her gait. But the mare wanted to play with her new friend. "Wish I had a saddle," he said.

"Yes, you would be pleased with the smooth ride she gives," the friend stated.

Joyce watched—not particularly impressed. She did remember the thrill of discovering a Fox Trotter's smooth motion, years earlier on one of Bob's geldings. Could this gray really be that smooth?

When they were home, Larry called the owner. He had difficulty getting much background information, but the price was fair. There would be no papers, as the mare had never been registered. Joyce didn't care about the papers. "She will be a good companion for your mare."

Larry took the mare to the stallion's barn where Carmen was. He had the breeder also ride her, to determine if her gait was true. He wanted her registered, and there was some urgency as 1980 was the last year to register a Fox Trotter on performance.

"Why is that so important?" Joyce asked. "I never intend to show her."

"If she is registered, her foals will automatically be. That's what I'm thinking about."

Joyce mused on that. She was learning so much about horses already.

The gray mare passed the performance test and the next decision was to name her, as they sent in the registration papers.

"Genesis seems appropriate. She's the first horse we've named. I'll call her Jennie. Jennie, my old gray mare," said Joyce.

When the breeding was completed, Bob and his horse trailer brought the mares to The Back 40. It was fun to actually have their own horses on the land.

Bob loaned Joyce an English saddle to try. She watched Jennie in action and then cautiously mounted her. The mare seemed to realize she was carrying a cautious person and took special care. Soon the easy walk became the fluid motion of a Trotter. There was little saddle action as Jennie and Joyce floated along.

Larry rode alongside. He had Carmen collected in the gait.

"Well, what do you think?"

"Oh, she's great," Joyce replied breathlessly.

"She acts as if she knows she is your horse." He moved out in front, as they crested a rise in the pasture.

Later, as they were brushing the mares, the western sky was ablaze with a true Kansas sunset. The golden rays caught in Jennie's slow, swishing, flaxen tail. It was a beautiful sight to Joyce.

When the school term started in the fall, a routine was established. Joyce and Larry left for the farm as soon as possible on Friday. Usually there was time for an evening ride before a late supper. Saturday was divided between projects, time with the horses, and friends who came to visit. They went home late Saturday night, so Larry would be ready to preach on Sunday mornings at an inner-city church where he was serving part-time as an interim pastor. Sunday afternoons they drove the forty-five miles again, for some precious time at the farm. All week they planned for the next weekend. The mares responded to the attention and would follow Joyce or Larry to the house. Jennie liked to stand and look in the back door.

Chapter Four

In December they moved the mares to a stable near the city. The retreat house was winterized and unused from January to March. Then, how good it was to take the mares home to The Back 40. They appeared to be happy, and settled in to await the foals. The weekend routine began again.

Their first foal was Magic, and now they had Little Bo Jangles. Life was full and fun.

Joyce never tired of just watching Jennie and Little Bo. He was alert, with those big, floppy ears tracing every sound. He was also curious and would leave Jennie's side to explore. Finally he would approach Joyce, and he soon learned the delightful taste of a sugar cube.

The two colts began to discover each other, playing and sparring together and nipping each other's necks. Magic was bigger, but Bo acted as his equal. In the early mornings they would romp and cavort while the mares placidly continued grazing. Soon they readily came up to anyone with apple and carrot treats.

After three weeks, the mares traveled back to the stallion's barn with their little colts accompanying them. This time, Jennie would be bred with Duke's Carbon Copy, another stallion of Bob's. She hated the barn confinement and was always anxious to leave it when Joyce arrived to take her out. Little Bo trotted up to any horse or person for attention. He even challenged the stallion across the fence until his dam called him back. Finally, the breeding was over and the mares and colts were returned to The Back 40.

Joyce and Bo Jangles (six months old)

Magic and Bo Jangles (six months old)

The horseback riding began again. It was more fun than before, with the little colts trotting happily along with their little tails lifted up like flags. The adjoining 160 acres were deserted now and open for riding. On horseback, they explored other bluffs and creeks. Larry and Joyce used the abandoned road to hold the mares in their gait.

The large one-room barn Larry had built began to look crowded, with the two mares and the growing colts. So Larry began an addition of a center hallway and three enclosed stalls across from the original barn. Stairs in one stall led to the loft over the hall. Now there was room for the hay that would be cut and stored.

The colts were beginning to seriously eat the oats, so it was good to have a stall for each. They quickly learned which stall to hurry to when they saw the oats coming. Like pets, they followed Joyce and Larry back to the house, sniffing out more treats.

During autumn, the leaves colored to all the rich amber and gold colors of hardwood trees. Both the riders and horses were eager to speed over the pastures or explore the bluffs and trails during those brisk, cooler days. Often, it was necessary to cross a creek. Bo could not resist extra splashing, and he and Magic were dripping by the time they reached the other side. It was always like a great adventure. Only during the last quarter of a mile to the barn did the little colt lag behind.

Bo's mane was thick and straight. It stood straight up, like a Roman soldier's helmet. He was growing a thick, furry coat. He and Magic began to look like woolly bears. Joyce was concerned.

"Do you think it's going to be a hard, cold winter? Their coats are so thick."

"They will be prepared for it. It's nature's way," Larry answered.

"Are we taking them all to the city this winter?"

"No, I think they'll be happier here. We'll ask George to feed them and check on them regularly."

"Oh, I hope it's mild enough for us to have our family

Christmas here. Christina and Steve will enjoy the horses so much."

"Yes, and then we'll have to think about weaning the colts. I don't think the mares will do it on their own."

Christmas was mild, with only light, dusting snow to collect in the ditches and along the road. It was fun to decorate the house in a festive manner. Joyce made little felt saddlebags to hang at the hearth. Larry brought in a cedar tree from the front pasture. Additional cedar boughs decked the front windows. How fragrant they smelled. It was all cheerful and cosy for the family. The horses enjoyed the extra attention and treats. It was possible to ride the mares, and the colts were beginning to respond to attempts to lead them around the farm.

Chapter Five

After the holidays, Larry looked at the calendar. "I have some time—some extra days off this last week of January. We'll plan to wean the colts then, if we don't have a bad storm."

"How will we separate them long enough?"

"I've asked the neighbor down the road if we can put the mares in his empty pasture. The colts will stay here."

"Alone? How long will it take?"

"A month at least, I think."

"What will happen when we bring the mares back? Will they get along?" Joyce worried.

"Yes, they should, but the relationship will be different," Larry answered.

Joyce looked at her growing black foal. "Oh, Little Bo, I wish you could stay this size forever."

Larry went down to the farm during the last week in January. He put the mares in stalls—allowing the foals to be near but not with their dams to nurse. By Friday evening, when Joyce arrived, the mares and colts were showing their displeasure. Also, a snowstorm was predicted.

"How is it going?" Joyce asked getting out of the car.

Larry helped unload groceries from her car. "No one is happy with me, that's for sure. The mares don't like being confined. They kicked the barn the first night. Their tits are getting tight, and they are uncomfortable."

"What about the colts?"

"They stay close to the partitions and are confused, but they're okay," he answered.

Later at the barn, while patting the little colt, Joyce held his head and said, "I'm sorry, Little Bo. I know you want your mama. But it's time for you to grow up."

The sky was overcast and threatening on Saturday. At noon, a light rain had turned to sleet. By the time friends had arrived to help, Joyce was not sure the plan was going to work.

Larry greeted Carol and Jake and gave instructions. "The colts are up by the barn. We'll stall them and then let the mares out. Hopefully they will let us ride them up to the neighbor's pasture."

"What do you want us to do?" Jake asked as Joyce noticed the sleet coming down harder.

"Stay with the colts. They will need reassuring. And then, if one of you could drive up the road to get us—okay?"

Everyone agreed to the plan. Jake gave Joyce his special rain gear to use. The mares were led reluctantly away to be saddled.

"Let's mount them and go right away, before they get more upset," Larry instructed as he helped Joyce up. The little colts could be heard whinnying, and the mares turned back toward the barn.

Jennie whirled twice with Joyce as she resisted the bit's pressure, telling her to go up the road away from the barn. Finally she took off in a trot behind Carmen. By the time they reached the outer gate, both mares were running full-out in panic. It was sleeting harder. Joyce wondered if she would be able to stop Jennie and held the reins tightly.

The mares raced on. The neighbor's pasture gate was open and Larry rode Carmen in without stopping, so Joyce followed on Jennie. Then, when the gate was closed, the mares finally halted and were unsaddled. They were still hyper and ran around all the fence border, looking for an escape. Larry walked the same path, checking to be sure the fence was secure.

Joyce herself was upset and wet when she loaded her saddle in Jake's car. *There has to be a better way,* she thought.

Before the end of the day, the sleet turned completely to snow. Freed from his stall, Little Bo was running in the pasture, calling for his mama.

After the first lonely days, the colts learned to fend for themselves, and almost appeared to enjoy the extra freedom to explore on their own. Bo became more assertive. Even though he and Magic played as equals, it was Bo who usually gave the signals to move Magic on. Both were growing fast.

The light snow swirled back and forth across the highway like waves. It was moved in one direction by the forceful wind and in the opposite direction by the traffic. The borderlines of the road were lost in the froth. White fields blended into the gray-white sky, almost resulting in a white-out. Larry drove steadily on. His intense eyes never left the highway. Joyce found comfort in watching his confident hands grip the black leather wheel. Occasionally lights of an approaching vehicle pierced the hazy white and then disappeared.

"Do you think we'll reach the farm before dark?"

"We should; we're making good time, despite the snow."

"It's still going to be difficult finding the colts. They'll never hear our whistle in this wind."

"It's a good thing they're black."

"Yes, Jennie will blend right in with the sky and snow. But Carmen will show up." Joyce flinched as she recognized a car in the ditch. Quickly it, too, was lost in the blowing snow. If the snow continued falling, the car would be half-buried by the morning, when the plows would come searching. She remembered seeing cars like that on the Colorado mountain roads—not in the Midwest.

The four-lane highway narrowed to only two lanes. That meant only ten more miles to go. Larry slowed the rate of the car. Joyce noticed the tension in his hands. She looked away.

I'll close my eyes, she thought, *and then we'll be there.*

After a few seconds, she decided *not* looking was worse, and opened her eyes. Silently they rode the last few miles. Larry turned off onto the blacktop, and then he was slowing at the gravel road. The wind appeared to blow with even more force.

"We'll go on to find the colts first," he said as he stopped at the gate. Joyce hopped out to open the gate.

The snow made the lane from the gate to the house impass-
ible. They parked the car and started walking. The snow was
eight inches deep, and higher in places where it was drifting.
It was hard to walk. The colts were not by the house or barn.
Their whistles only died in the wind or blew back in their faces.
Finally they separated, each taking a different route. At last
Joyce found the two shivering colts down the bluff, where they
were somewhat protected from the wind. She led them back to
the barn and rang the bell to alert Larry. He was soon there
to help feed and rub the colts. Joyce poured hot water into the
feed tubs filled with the oats and stirred briskly. Larry began
to let hay down from the loft.

"There you are, Bo Jangles. Let's get your circulation going.
Larry, will they be all right?"

"Sure, they are healthy, and they've had their shots. This
is a bad storm, though, so we need to be sure they get enough
oats and hay."

Once the colts' appetites were somewhat appeased, they
began to run and frisk around in the snow. It was a pleasure
to watch the little black shapes against the white background.

On the way home, it was easy to find the mares waiting
by the fence of the neighbor's pasture. They were anxious for
the oats.

The snow continued to fall during the night. The temperature remained below freezing, but the following days were
windless and sunny. Sometimes it was harder to find the colts,
as they roamed in the sun on the other side of the field. But
once they heard the familiar whistle, they would come flying
over the snow.

Joyce often drove the forty miles alone when Larry was
busy. She would be breathless from walking through the deep
drifts.

"You may never be a big horse, Bo Jangles, but I know you
will be a beautiful horse. You are so black and shiny. And I
hope you will never lose your playfulness," Joyce added as she
tramped through the snow with the frisky colt.

"I saw your mama today and told her you were fine. I'm

sure she's proud of your taking care of yourself." Bo lifted his head and pranced along as if to confirm her opinion. His thick black mane was finally bending to turn over and it ruffled in the breeze.

After five weeks of separation, Larry walked the mares back home. Joyce was waiting with the colts at the gate, anxious to witness the reunion. The colts caught site of the mares as they hurried up to the gate with Larry. Bo was standing still and alert. Suddenly Joyce thought he looked older and more mature. What was he thinking?

Jennie pushed through the gate, and Bo rushed over to her. She turned sharply to forestall him from nursing and headed for the barn. He looked confused and tried twice more to head her off, by walking around in front of her, so he could nurse. Each time he met with the same warning from her. Without stopping, she went up the hill to the barn.

Magic was getting the same response from Carmen. Puzzled and dejected, the colts followed the mares to the barn and went into their own feeding stalls.

In a few days, Bo understood the new rules Jennie imposed. The mare and colt were compatible, but the loving mare-foal relationship was over. The comfort of nursing would no longer be available. Bo and Magic stayed near the mares in the pasture, but they were freer to go for runs by themselves.

Chapter Six

Larry looked at the calendar again and marked a week in March. It was the week both he and Joyce had as a spring vacation from teaching. Across that week of March he wrote "gelding."

Fortunately, the end of March was mild. Winter had not retired from the Midwest, but it appeared she would take a rest and not disturb the sunny week.

The veterinarian came and performed the castration of the colts without any difficulty. They were sedated, and he operated on them outside the barn in the new budding grass. Little Bo recovered quickly and was walking around with little difficulty.

"I hope you won't mind not being a stallion," Joyce whispered to Bo as she fed him pieces of carrot. "This way, you'll be free in a field and not always have to stay in a barn stall." Little Bo did not know what it would mean not to be free—free to run, jump, explore, and graze at will.

With spring arriving, the riding could begin again. Now, Bo and Magic raced across the field—always ahead of the mares. One would chase the other, until they both would rear up and spar like stallions. They were yearlings, now.

When May came, Larry began to speculate on when the mares would foal again. The colts were put out in the front pasture, so they would not disturb the mares.

Carmen had gained weight, but the vet confirmed Larry's fears that it was not because she was still with foal. It was a disappointment, but always a possibility with foaling.

Another school year ended on June third, and as soon as responsibilities ended and reports were completed, Joyce met Larry to drive to the farm. As they walked up the hill to the barn, they saw a new little foal lift up its head as if to say "hello."

"A filly! We have a filly," Larry exclaimed.

"She's so much bigger than Bo Jangles was."

They watched as the day-old filly ran around her mama in larger and larger circles, until Jennie voiced her displeasure. Then she trotted back to stand by her dam. She was eager to make friends with Joyce and Larry right away. In the barn, as Joyce knelt down to be at eye level, the little filly climbed right into her arms.

Jennie was having problems though. Carmen was jealously trying to get to the filly to claim her as her own. When the vet arrived later, he observed this behavior and told Larry he'd have to separate the mares. So, the next morning Carmen was loaded into the horse trailer to go back to the stallion's barn.

Then Jennie could relax with her new foal. Joyce named the new filly with the white star "Jennie's Joy."

Meanwhile, Bo and Magic kept as close a watch as possible through the separating fence. The third day, Larry led them into the back pasture by the barn to begin getting acquainted with the little foal. They slunk in together, looking like two awkward adolescents. Jennie kept her ears back as if to say, "That's close enough." The daily visit became a morning routine, and each day their time together was lengthened.

Finally, Larry felt the colts could be trusted to be left with Jennie and her new filly. So Joyce went to the front pasture to find them. Magic and Bo came running when they heard the familiar whistle. Joyce's pleasure at watching them turned to panic when she noticed Bo's injury. What had happened to his foot? It was all bloody! Quickly she found Larry. After one quick appraisal, he haltered Bo, led him to the barn, and stalled him. Joyce stayed with Bo, while Larry drove off to get the vet.

Somehow, Little Bo had cut his back right hoof below the pastern. It was a deep, ugly cut and in a difficult place. It could not be stitched shut. Each time he moved, the lower part of his hoof dangled loosely. Fortunately, no tendons had been severed. At first, the vet suggested trying to see how it would heal on its own if Bo stayed in the stall. When he returned on the third day and the gash remained as deep and ugly, he reversed his decision. Carefully, he lifted up the little bloody hoof and wound the injury with a pressure bandage.

Joyce watched the bandage being tightly bound and fastened.

"Do you have any idea if it will heal right?"

"Well, it's a deep cut in a bad place. We'll watch it closely and continue to wrap it with tighter and tighter pressure bandages. He has to stay in the stall."

Joyce looked sympathetically at the restless colt and wondered if he'd ever fly across the pasture again. Then she heard Larry ask the vet if he had any idea how long it might take for the foot to heal.

The vet collected his equipment and began walking to his truck. "We'll start with two weeks in mind. But I'll be back every three days, at first, to change and tighten the bandage." He looked across the pasture at Jennie and her new filly. "Your new little foal looks as if she is doing okay."

"Yes, and we moved the other mare. I guess we are finding out that anything can happen with horses—good and bad."

After the vet had driven off, Joyce stood by the stall, stroking the little black gelding. Larry was near, almost absentmindedly rubbing behind Magic's ear. Magic had spent a lot of time in the barn hall the last three days, near his friend, wondering why he couldn't come out to play. Joyce turned to look at Larry.

"I really feel terrible about this. I wonder if we will ever know how he was hurt."

"Probably not. We do need to change our schedules, so someone can always be down at The Back 40 to feed and take care of him. I'm sure George will help."

"Yes, but I'm free now with school over. I can stay most of the time. Your summer term will begin before the two weeks are up."

The two weeks extended into six long and frustrating weeks for Joyce and Little Bo. Just as it appeared as if the injury was healing, it would break open again. Bo would get very restless and paw and stamp his feet. He did not like being alone in the barn. Both hall doors of the barn were left open, and occasionally the other horses would stand in there with him. But then they would go back out again to graze, and he would neigh his displeasure. Joyce could hear him from the house and would run up to the barn with a carrot. She fed and watered him three times a day and kept him in a clean stall.

At first, Bo did not eat or drink well. Joyce began going out early each morning to cut and bring in long grass and sweet clover.

"Good morning, Little Bo. Here you are. Yes, I thought you'd like this clover. You miss grazing, don't you? Ahh, Little Bo, don't be sad. You'll be okay soon. And besides, I love you."

Her words seemed to soothe him. Certainly her presence did. She spent hours in the barn, talking to the yearling and trying to amuse him. She took a radio to the barn, thinking that would provide company when she was away. But he was frightened by the strange noises he couldn't identify, no matter where she placed the radio or what station she tried.

The vet came regularly. Joyce was always relieved when another person was there to help hold Bo as the bandage was removed and the foot treated and rebound. One evening, she held tightly to the rope as the vet began snipping at the bandage. Bo was not cooperative. Finally, he reared and burst through the stall gate, leaving Joyce and the vet on the ground. Then, after tasting his freedom for a short run, he allowed Joyce to lead him back into a different, more secure, stall.

"Did he do any more damage with all that activity?" she asked, as once again she held the rope.

"I don't think so, but it's not healing very quickly." He stood up after collecting his instruments and bandages. "Well, it will just take a little longer." The next time the vet came, he brought his teenage son to hold the rope.

By the fourth week, Joyce was driving back and forth from

the city to meet obligations she had there. She was grateful to their neighbor, George, who came to feed and water Bo. But she was always anxious to return to the barn herself, because she knew how lonely he was. Larry would help out on the weekends.

One Saturday, after giving the barn a thorough cleaning, he commented, "This is taking longer than we'd hoped. How are you doing?"

"Oh, I'm okay, when I'm not worrying if the foot will ever be healed right."

"Your Bo has been worrying about it all, too."

"How can you tell? What do you mean?"

"See those light rings showing up on his hooves? Those are stress signs. They'll grow out eventually—like fingernails. But the distance they are now show how much they've grown since the trauma of the accident and being stalled."

"Poor Little Bo. You are being brave, aren't you?"

July brought hot, muggy weather. The breeze that had cooled the barn hall stilled. Joyce began to get up earlier in the mornings to cut the clover and complete the barn duties. Then she would feed and enjoy playing with the new filly. Her attention always returned to the little black gelding looking wistfully over his stall gate.

Finally, the vet said it was time to leave the bandage off.

"The cut needs air, to complete healing on its own."

"It still looks pretty raw," Joyce replied doubtfully. "Are you sure?"

"The foot may look worse before it looks better. But we have to try. Now, do you think you can treat the cut three times a day with this?" He held out a bottle of purple liquid with a dauber.

"I'll try," Joyce said quietly.

After the vet had driven away, she was even less sure of successfully treating the wound. Bo would begin to dance around in the stall if he thought she was even looking at his foot. Joyce was painfully aware of her lack of experience with horses before Jennie.

George and Almeda came that afternoon to check on Bo's progress. Joyce showed them the medicine.

"I'm not having very good luck treating the injury with this. I don't want to hurt him. And yet, I know how important it is."

The sympathetic neighbors watched the restless colt and thought it might be dangerous for Joyce to bend over in the stall with Bo to treat the foot. After a short time, during which Joyce and George had little success actually applying the purple dauber to the cut, Almeda said she had an idea and hurried home. When she returned, she had a little, toy, plastic water gun.

"This might work," she said. "My grandsons left this at our house. Maybe you could squirt the medicine on the injury from a safe distance out of the stall."

Joyce and George laughed, but allowed Almeda to fill the toy gun with the purple medicine. George took aim.

"Bull's eye," he shouted.

"Hooray," Joyce joined. "And Bo didn't even know anything happened."

Joyce kept the toy gun and practiced on a rock target. Even so, her aim was not always as direct as George's had been. But the cut was treated. The purple stain made it easy to see where her shot landed.

The vet was amused. "Well, anything that works. Now, I think we can let this little fellow have a taste of freedom."

"Really? You mean, let him out of the stall?"

"Not until tomorrow morning—oh, about eleven o'clock when the grass is dry. He can't go out when the grass is wet or he might get dew poison. Keep him in the back pasture and put him back in the stall for the nights."

Joyce could hardly sleep that night. She listened to the whippoorwills and thought, *Is it too soon? Will he open the cut again? How will I ever catch him to put him back in the stall?*

Early the next morning, she began the usual routine. Her hands were shaky, but she squirted the purple medicine on the first try.

"Oh, do I have a surprise for you," she sang as she measured out the oats. Little Bo craned his neck as he peered over the stall gate to watch her in the feed room of the barn. By 9:00 A.M. the oats and clover were eaten and the stall clean, with fresh straw. The next two hours dragged. Joyce kept going out to feel if the grass was still moist. Finally, about eleven o'clock, Joyce went out and felt the pasture grass for the last time. The hot sun had dried away all traces of the night's dew. She walked back through the barn hall to Bo's stall.

"Okay, my friend, this is the moment we've been waiting for. Take care now—easy does it." She slid open the stall gate. Bo came out and started to walk back to the other stall he sometimes used. But that stall gate was closed. Bo waited, but instead of being pulled into a stall, he felt the pressure released, as Joyce let go of his halter and stood back. He looked at her, waited a moment, and turned around. He took a few steps, then stopped again and turned to look back at her.

"That's right—go ahead, now; just be careful." She held her breath. He took a few more steps, and again stopped to check. And then, as the full realization hit him, Bo began moving faster out of the barn hall—out, to be free!

For ten minutes, Joyce watched spellbound, as the black gelding ran, jumped, kicked, rolled, and cavorted for joy. He barely touched the ground as he celebrated freedom. The other horses watched from across the pasture.

Joyce was crying and laughing at the same time. It was a time of pure, shared ecstasy. All the pent-up emotions of the last six weeks were finally being spent for both of them.

Bo finally rolled and stood up to shake off the dust. Then he moved in a slower, easier gait. Joyce ran to him and hugged his neck. He allowed her to stroke him as she checked the foot. It was okay. "Thank God!"

Then she stood back. "Go on. Go find Magic. Mr. Bo Jangles, you are free!"

The other horses were up by the fence. Bo trotted up to them, only to be met with rejection. Each time he got close, the horses laid their ears back and reached out as if to nip. He was puzzled and soon stayed at a safe distance. He was happy to be free, but he needed companionship. Bo returned to Joyce and stayed at her side, as she walked around the pasture.

"It's not fair," she said later to Larry when Bo was back in the stall for the night. "Why do they treat him that way?"

"It's a horse's lot to always have to work his way back into a herd, no matter how large or small that herd is—or if the herd in question is his mother, sister, and best friend."

"You're sounding like a professor. This is not funny."

Larry smiled and gave her a hug. "I know, and you've done a good job with Bo. Be patient; it won't take long."

The next morning Bo ate his oats, but left some of the clover, as he was anxious to be free again. When released, he ran and jumped again, though not as energetically as he had on the previous morning. Joyce watched as the distance between Bo and Magic lessened, and soon the two of them were sparring. "Oh, be careful, Little Bo," she whispered.

By the time the vet gave his okay for Bo to stay out at night, he and Magic were close buddies again. Bo still trailed close behind Joyce whenever she was out in the pasture. Then he'd follow her back down the hill to the house, with his little hooves clicking out the broken-gait rhythm. Magic began to follow too. Joyce loved giving carrot and apple pieces to them from the back stoop of the house.

One day, while she was treating and playing with the yearlings, she saw the new filly watching from the top of the path. With a little encouragement she approached the others, ate a carrot and stayed to be included. Often after that Joyce would see the filly with the geldings in their playing. The yearlings appeared to instinctively know to be more gentle with her.

Carmen returned, and the five settled into an easygoing herd. Now, when Larry and Joyce rode the mares, there were three happy young horses trotting along. The geldings would begin to chase the little filly, and she would fly over the field and kick up her heels. Always, right before it looked like Bo or Magic would catch her, the filly would dart behind Jennie. Then, with her head high and nostrils flaring, she would prance in her special springy little gait. Like the yearlings, she held her tail high. It was full and looked like a plume. A tired, happy trio followed the mares after a ride back to the barn.

Larry was out of town on the weekend of Joyce's birthday. She went alone on that Friday to be at The Back 40 with the horses. She fed them in the barn and stayed up in the pasture with them until the sun had set. Then she went down the hill to the house to fix her own supper. As she was clearing the dishes, she heard a sound at the back door. Looking out, she saw Little Bo standing outside, alone, as if he were waiting for her to come out. Grabbing the ever-ready carrot, she went to join him in the circle drive by the hitching post.

It was a beautiful, clear, warm night with an almost-full moon and stars shining bright. The black horse blended in with the night. He seemed to want to play. Joyce fed him the carrot and took a few steps. So did he. Then she skipped around in a circle. He imitated her movements. She backed up. He followed. The next half hour was spent in a sort of follow-the-leader game for just the two of them. Joyce stopped to catch her breath.

"Oh, Little Bo, you are something else. What a fun way to spend my birthday evening. You are making it so special!"

She sat on the stoop and he came nearer so she could reach to stroke behind his ear. They remained in silence until she finally looked into his eyes and said, "If anyone had told me I would be doing this on my forty-ninth birthday, I would have never believed them. I can't think of anywhere I would rather be. Will we be together again next year for my big one? Maybe then I can ride you. Little Bo, I love you!"

Bo Jangles, looking for a carrot

Chapter Seven

Another Christmas was celebrated at The Back 40, with three generations of family present.

In January, Joyce noticed Larry looking at the calendar again.

"What are you planning for, now?"

"Two things, actually. The filly, Joy, needs to be weaned, and it's time to think about training the colts."

"Are we taking Jennie away again?"

"No, I think we'll take the filly to the city stables with the colts. They can be trained there and be company for Joy. Only the mares will stay here."

Joyce looked at the five horses grazing up by the fence. This January's weather had started out milder. The sun was setting. As always, the sun's rays caught the movement of Jennie's flaxen tail, resulting in sparkling highlights. Joy was nursing.

"They all look so peaceful. I wish it could stay this way."

But she knew it was time to begin the gelding's training to encourage the smooth Fox Trotter's broken gait for riding. And the little filly seemed happy with the geldings. She certainly tried to do whatever they did.

It rained hard during the month of February and, twice, plans to load and move the three young horses had to be cancelled. The horse trailer mired in the mud. Finally, in March, there was a break in the weather.

Larry spent a most frustrating afternoon trying to get Magic into the trailer. He simply could not be coaxed to step in.

The next morning, Larry parked the trailer at the end of the barn hall and again, with Joyce holding out Magic's tub of oats, Larry tried to coax and push the gelding in. Magic was not cooperative, even though he wanted the oats that were just out of reach.

The mares were in stalls, so Jennie could not nurse the filly. But Bo and Joy were in the barn hall at the other end. Suddenly, during a break in the futile effort with Magic, the filly walked up to the trailer, hopped in, and began to eat Magic's oats. Bo was quick to join her. Recovering from surprise, Larry quickly closed the trailer doors and secured the horses inside.

"This isn't the order I'd planned to take them in, but it's a full trailer, so I'll not complain."

Joyce helped secure Bo and Joy's halters to the trailer, got them more oats and hay, and released the mares from their stalls before getting in the car beside Larry. Magic was left standing alone in the barn hall as Bo and Joy were starting their adventure to the city.

The two horses were taken to the boarding stables Larry and Joyce owned with their friends, Bob and Jan. When they reached their destination, Larry gently coaxed them out of the trailer.

Everything was strange and different. There were more people and more horses around. Bo and Joy were skittish, as Larry and Joyce led them to a small pasture behind the large boarding barn. There they could be alone. Bo seemed to sense he was the filly's protector. He always positioned himself between her and any person or animal. He stood close to her so she could rest her head on him. All during the first long, dark night he kept this vigil.

Chapter Eight

Soon the two young horses adjusted to the new environment and routine. Bo's initial training began under the gentle but firm hands of Dennis, the trainer. Bo appeared to like this attention and would try to respond to whatever the tugging straps commanded him to do. The filly was desolate when left alone for even a short time and would call to Bo and try to break through the pasture fence. Finally, she was brought in the barn also and stalled near the indoor arena, so she could see him during the training sessions.

By the second week, Dennis was on Bo and riding him each evening, 'round and 'round the indoor arena. There were usually several other riders encouraging their two-year-old Fox Trotters into their unique walk and finally into the fox-trot. Joyce stood stroking the filly behind her ear as she watched Bo reach for a longer stride.

"He's responsive," Dennis said. "He moves into the walk naturally, but it will take time to confirm the fox-trot." That was the longest speech Joyce had heard from Dennis. *Bo must be doing well,* she thought. Dennis rode by again.

"Do you want to try him?"

"Oh no, not yet." She turned to Larry. "You try him."

So, with a different rider, Bo began to walk and then trot around that arena circle again. Later Dennis suggested, "You might increase his daily ration of oats. He is developing strong muscles."

Bob was in the barn, evenings now, trying to confirm his four-year-old stallion. Son was a beautiful, large, black stallion.

His performance looked good to Joyce, but she knew he had not placed well as a two- or three-year-old.

After Bob had released Son back into his stall, he would stand at the arena gate and watch Little Bo. Bob was wearing the face mask he always wore in the barn now. The doctor thought a persistent cough he had could be due to a hay allergy.

"I'm more impressed with your Bo all the time. Are you planning to enter him in competition?"

"No, not really. Do you think he would be ready this year?"

"He's coming along well in both the walk and fox-trot. Two-year-olds don't canter." Then , after a short time of watching Bo go around for Dennis, Bob added, "I'd like to ride him for you. I think he could be a winner."

Joyce spent fewer evenings at the barn, as she was more occupied with her work and other activities. Larry would often stop by the barn on the way home from the seminary and watch Bo's progress. Finally, he had been able to haul Magic from The Back 40. Dennis had suggested delaying Magic's training, as he felt he was still in the process of growing and his back legs weren't strong enough.

Dennis completed his training of Bo, and Bob began riding the little gelding regularly. As spring approached, with warmer weather, the training could be moved to the larger outdoor arena. Bob liked Bo's quick snappy steps and added jingles to his bridle to pick up the sound of the rhythm. He selected a show in mid-May to be the first entry for Bo Jangles. The Friday night before the show, Bob and Jan showed how the special grooming was done. When Bo was all clean and brushed, the new gold horse blanket was tied on to keep him clean, and he was put in a stall for the night.

Saturday morning Joyce woke Larry up to a cold and rainy day. She thought about Bob's persistent cough and cold.

"Do you think the show will be cancelled?"

Larry answered as he tugged on his boots, "No, it's all inside. Once we get Bo there, we'll be fine." He left for the barn to help Bob load and take Bo to the location of the show. Joyce left later and drove straight to the show barn to meet them.

She was surprised the horse van was not yet there but went on inside to watch the preshow activities. Demonstrations on horse care and showing were taking place. Also, a lady was demonstrating how to braid the fancy ribbons the horses wore in their forelock and manes. Joyce was glad Jan had supplied Bo with a set and would tie them on this first time.

At the end of the preshow there was still no sign of the red van. The first show classes would start soon, and many of the riders were taking advantage of the last opportunity to warm up their horses in the arena ring.

Finally, across the ring, Joyce saw Larry leading Bo into the building. The groomed black gelding looked sharp in his gold horse blanket and leg wraps. Joyce hurried around the track to meet them. Larry looked worried.

"You're late. I was getting concerned."

"We had a mishap on the way, but I think everything is okay now."

"What happened? Where's Bob?"

"He's out parking the van and will bring in his saddle and tack." He reached the indoor stall reserved for Bo, and stopped for Joyce to undo the latch. Then he asked, "Do you notice any limp?"

"Any limp? What do you mean? What happened, Larry?"

Larry leaned over to take off the leg wrappings. Joyce noticed he was carefully feeling the front legs. He finished, straightened up, and said, "Bo Jangles loaded well, and we started out in good time. But we were only a few miles away from the stable and going around a curve, when we could feel Bo shift his weight. We heard a thump, and I stopped the car. Bob hurried out to check the hitch. I ran around back and noticed one door looked warped. Bo seemed okay. Then I knelt down and looked under the trailer and saw a board hanging down.

"I realized that the trailer flooring had broken through and that Bo had somehow jumped back to keep his front legs from going through."

"Oh, no," Joyce whispered in horror.

"He appeared unhurt. As we were checking him out, a passing truck stopped. The driver had a piece of plywood that I used to temporarily repair the floor. Bob and I decided to come on and try him out. I'll have to secure that flooring before we haul him back."

"But Bo's all right, isn't he? He wasn't limping." She remembered he hadn't even limped with his bad injury the year before. She turned to greet Bob, who had arrived with his saddle. He answered her question. "We'll check him out in the ring. I want to warm him up before the judging classes begin."

Bo stood almost at attention as he was saddled and bridled. Jan tied on the blue- and gold-braided ribbons. Then Bob led him to the arena. Bo was not limping.

But, as soon as Bob mounted and began urging Bo to move forward, the gelding began to favor a front leg. Halfway around the ring, he was limping noticeably. As Joyce watched, she remembered the injured foot of a year earlier and wanted to cry. She met Bob at the far side of the arena as he dismounted and unsaddled Bo.

"I'm sorry, Joyce. He can't be ridden today."

"What can I do for him?"

Bob swung the saddle over his shoulder and handed Joyce the reins. "Just walk him over here out of the way. You want to keep the leg from getting stiff."

Left alone with Bo, Joyce stroked his neck and said softly, "Well, here we are again, Bo Jangles, you and me." They walked back and forth. Each time a new class of horses entered the arena, Bo would perk up his ears and look questioningly, as if to ask, "When is it going to be my turn?"

Finally, Joyce led him back to his stall and gave him hay. Larry and Bob were watching the other horses perform. Joyce's only concern was the little gelding. "Don't worry, Bo Jangles. You'll get your chance some other day."

Larry had repaired the floor of the horse trailer. It was time to take Bo back to the stable. Bob and Jan were staying on, as she was helping with concessions, and Bob was helping with traffic in the parking lot. Jan was upset Bob wasn't wearing a warmer jacket. He assured her he was fine, before walking back out into the rainy weather.

The return trip to the stables was uneventful, and Bo was happy to be free to roll over again. Larry treated the front legs with DMSO and told the barn manager he'd check on the horse the next afternoon.

Leaving the stables, Joyce and Larry drove to The Back 40 to rest and check on the mares. Carmen was due to foal soon. Jennie had not been bred to foal after her two successive pregnancies.

Chapter Nine

They arrived at the farm in the late afternoon. The rain had stopped. As soon as the car was unloaded, Larry headed for the barn.

Joyce called after him. "I'm going to lie down. I'll only go to the barn if you need me, or if there is a new foal to see."

She went inside. Before she had her boots off, Larry came running to the house.

"Come and see. Carmen had her new colt!"

Forgetting she was tired, Joyce ran up the hill after him.

The joy of caring for the new colt, which they called Sam, brought back all the fun memories of Bo and the other foals. Joyce spent more time at the farm as the school year ended.

Back at the stables near the city, Bob began slowly to exercise Bo Jangles. There was no permanent injury, and the vet declared he could be ridden again. Bob began working him for a show in June. This time, Larry decided to enter Joy, the filly, in a model class. For a model class, the horses were only led around the ring and judged on appearance and conformation. So, a yearling could be entered.

The Saturday in June was bright and sunny. Both Bo Jangles and Joy were groomed and loaded into the van that had a new flooring. The trip to the show was without incident.

This show was a larger outdoor affair, with many horses of many different breeds. After being unloaded, the horses sensed the excitement of the place. The filly, Joy, tried to stay close to Bo Jangles, her security. Larry led her away to walk, so Bob could saddle and begin to ride Bo. It was possible to warm up the horses in the large grassy area surrounding the three show rings that had classes going simultaneously.

After warming up Bo, Bob dismounted and handed Joyce the reins. He quickly saddled and mounted his stallion, Son, who would be entered in a later class.

Soon it was time for Larry to show the filly. Joyce tried to watch from a distance as she walked Bo Jangles.

Larry led Joy into the ring after the other four horses in this model class. Just as he reached the gate, a tractor started up nearby. The filly jumped and knocked Larry's hat off. Retrieving his hat, he tried to calm her and urged her on to catch up to the other horses. Halfway around the ring, Joy missed Bo and gave her special whinny for him. Joyce held Bo at a distance as he recognized and answered the filly's distressed call. Larry kept the filly walking, but she continued to call for her Bo. She did stop as the class lined up before the judges. Two larger more mature Fox Trotters took the blue and red ribbons. Then Jennie's Joy was called, and Larry walked her to collect the gold ribbon from the judge, as he led the filly from the ring.

Bob had mounted Bo again and was coaxing him into his gait as the larger class for two- and three-year-old Fox Trotters was announced. Back at the trailer, the filly continued to call for Bo as she munched on the hay. Joyce secured her to the trailer, gave her a final "be good" pat, and hurried to the ring to watch Bo Jangles perform.

Like the filly, Bo was the smallest horse in the class. Joyce tried to watch all the horses, to gain an understanding of the required performance of the fox-trot walk and gait. Most of the time, however, she only looked at the snappy little gelding with the jingles on his bridle. His walk was steady, but even she could see the fox-trot was not always smooth, as Bob gently urged him to move out. The horses went around the ring counter-clockwise many times, and then clockwise, before the judge told the riders to line up for the judging.

Bo Jangles did not place. Bob rode him out of the ring, handed Joyce the reins with a smile, before hurrying to mount Son for the next class.

"It's okay; he'll do better next time. Remember, this was his first competition."

Left with Bo, Joyce looked at him and said, "Ah, well, Bo Jangles, I thought you looked great out there. You know, I don't think I should call you Little Bo anymore either." The excited gelding pranced alongside as she led him back to the trailer where the anxious filly waited. She fed him carrot bits and thought he was certainly the handsomest horse at the show. So what if the judges hadn't agreed—this time.

After the horses were loaded up and being driven back to the stable, Joyce let out a sigh and said to Larry, "What an effort these shows are. I'd rather be on the farm, riding free."

"I know," he answered. "But he is getting good experience. I'm grateful Bob wants to ride him."

"Well, I don't understand the judging. Particularly when they only awarded Bob's stallion a fourth place. Maybe he won't want to show the horses again."

But the next day Bob was riding Bo and talking about the next show that would be in two weeks.

Joyce was hesitant—partly because Bo Jangles was coughing. The vet came and prescribed shots of penicillin to be administered for ten days. He had a bad respiratory infection that he had probably picked up from another horse at the show. Bob continued to ride Bo, but didn't work him as hard. Joyce and Jan watched one evening as Bob had Bo moving smoothly around the practice ring.

Joyce asked, "Can you tell if a horse is in a true fox-trot?"

Jan answered, "Watch his tail. It should make a smooth S as he goes by."

Joyce watched. As Bo went by the next time, his tail flowed in a perfect S. Then she commented, "I don't see how you and Bob kept up the schedule of the shows when he rode and modeled his two champions a couple of years ago."

Jan replied with a smile, "It was an effort—particularly if there were two or three shows a weekend. But Bob's always had so much energy. This year, though, that nagging cough just won't go away."

"Has he been to the doctor again?"

"Yes, he finally went. He's on some antibiotics."

The weekend of the next show arrived. Joyce and Larry were back at the stables grooming Bo. Then, with Jan and Bob, they were pulling Bo Jangles and Son to the show up north of the river. This would be an evening competition.

Riding in the car, Bob was excited. "Last night that little guy was the best ever. I could feel him stride like his daddy could. If we can just hold that gait."

They arrived at the fairgrounds where the show had already started. Jan told Joyce the show was classified as a "society show." That explained the accompanying organ music.

As always, there was a hustle to unload the horses, saddle them, and have them ready for Bob to warm up. Jan's steady fingers secured the ribbons she'd braided.

"You do that so well," Joyce remarked.

"Just practice," Jan replied.

Bo Jangle's class consisted of thirteen two- and three-year-olds. Again he was one of the smallest, but he was performing with more confidence and looked good.

Joyce and Jan stood at the show ring.

"What do you think?" Joyce asked anxiously as the horses seemed to glide past to the organ music.

"Watch the judges. See who they are looking at. Now, one is writing on his chart after studying Bo. That's a good sign."

"Oh, look. He coughed and stumbled a step!"

"Don't worry. The judges didn't see. He's fine now. Keep it up, Bo."

Joyce was almost too excited to keep watching. She saw Larry across the ring watching intently. The class seemed to last forever. Bo coughed one more time, but luckily was out of the judges' view again.

Finally, a judge motioned the riders to line up. Bo was standing alert as the judges checked the horses for the final time before giving the results to the Master of Ceremonies.

Then, after a fanfare by the organist, the winners were announced. Joyce had her fingers crossed like a little child. The blue and red ribbons were awarded.

"Third place goes to Jennie's Bo Jangles, owned by Joyce Wagley and ridden by Bob Carrigan!"

Joyce whooped with abandoned delight, as Bob moved Bo Jangles to the lady holding out the gold ribbon. Then she and Jan hurried to the arena gate to meet Bob. He was smiling broadly.

"He performed well."

"I agree!" Joyce took the reins and led Bo back to the trailer, praising him all the way. "Bo Jangles, you were terrific out there. Aren't you proud?" The gelding continued to step smartly by her side, as if he were still in the ring.

Joyce unsaddled Bo, exchanged a halter for the bridle, and began brushing him briskly as he began to munch on the hay. Bob had Son saddled and began to ride him for the last warm-up. "Be sure to walk him to help him cool down."

"I will, and good luck with Son."

Walking Bo around the outskirts of the arena, Joyce could see Bob riding the black stallion in the ring. This class had over twenty-four entries. Son did not place. Bob rode back to the trailer and began brushing Son. All four worked quickly to put away the tack and secure the horses in the trailer.

Joyce handed Bob a piece of pie and the chocolate she always gave him for riding Bo. "I don't understand. Son looks so good to me."

"Well, we are doing something wrong. I need to have a trainer come watch me ride Son, to help me know what that is." Finishing the pie, he smiled. "But your Bo was certainly performing well. That made my night." *What a dear friend,* Joyce thought.

Riding home, Larry and Bob reviewed the show and talked about plans for the stables. Bob was coughing again, but shrugged it off, saying he hadn't been wearing his face mask all the time in the barn. Joyce noticed Jan looked concerned and asked, "Have you checked with the doctor again?"

Jan answered for Bob, "No, but I think he should, as he is more congested in the mornings." She continued, "Maybe I'll make an appointment for him next week. I'll be leaving in about ten days to visit my mother in Ohio.”

“Yes, you told me that earlier. Anything I can do while you are gone?” Joyce asked.

“Just keep an eye on Bob. He may need to be reminded to take his medicine.”

“Well, I think he should slow down, particularly since he’ll be busy teaching his summer school classes.”

Chapter Ten

Larry and Bob were both teaching full time in the seminary's summer program. Jan left for Ohio, and Joyce went to the stable each day to check everything and spend time with the horses. She was anxious to ride Bo, but didn't want to interrupt the training program. Bob continued to ride Bo each evening. Often, it would be quite late before he led the gelding out to the lighted outdoor arena.

One evening, Larry told Joyce that Bob wanted to take Bo to another show the coming weekend. Joyce wasn't sure.

"He's so busy, and it's so hot now. Why do we need to do that? I'm more than pleased with the riding he's done."

"I know. I am too and told him so. But he really thinks Bo should be in this show. It has a class only for two-year-olds, so Bo would not have to compete with older, more experienced three-year-olds."

"I'd like to see how he'd do with only two-year-olds. But he's still not up to par, and Bob isn't feeling any better. I can tell he is pushing to get through his schedule as it is."

"True. But Bob isn't riding Bo too hard. I think the gelding is doing better. And Bob is taking some new medicine. The doctor now thinks he may have been allergic to some of the previous medicine."

Joyce remained doubtful about going to the show. Bob persisted, and finally, on Friday, Joyce agreed. At least the show was in the evening. Maybe it would be cooler. However, the first weekend in July was always hot in Kansas City.

The temperature was in the nineties, but a breeze was blowing as they drove the trailer with only Bo Jangles through the fairground's gate. This was a big show, with many classes, and it looked well attended.

Joyce had difficulty tying the ribbons on. "Tell Jan we needed her," she said as Bob mounted and began to ride.

Joyce enjoyed watching the show in progress. One class featured the total appearance of horse and rider to depict a certain period or effect. Two women were dressed in nineteenth-century gowns, riding sidesaddle. She wondered how hard that would be.

Others were dressed in Indian garb, cowboy clothes, and even a Raggedy Ann and Raggedy Andy were riding in a little cart pulled by two ponies. The crowd appreciated this effort of both horse and rider.

Bob was riding Bo Jangles in the warm-up ring. Bo was not doing well.

Larry walked up to Joyce, as the two-year-old class was going into the show ring. Joyce was fretting.

"He's not keeping the gait. Even I can tell that." She worried further. "I think his cough is returning."

Larry tried to be reassuring. "Maybe he'll turn on in the show ring."

It was not a large class—only five horses and riders. Even with only two-year-old Fox Trotters, Bo was the smallest.

However, it was not his size but rather his performance that hindered him. His fox-trot gait was not smooth, and he began to cough repeatedly. Each time he did that, he would stumble. Before the judges called for the horses to line up, Joyce could see even Bob looked strained. She only wanted it to be over, and wondered if Bob would signal to the judge to disqualify them. Then the horses were lining up. It was no surprise that Bo came out with the pink, fifth-place ribbon.

Both Bo Jangles and Bob were coughing, as they went back to the trailer.

"I don't know what happened," Bob said. "Neither of us was up to par."

"Well, I want a picture of you two anyway. I've never had

Bob on Bo Jangles at last Fox Trotter show

the chance before." She snapped two shots quickly, before Bob dismounted. He leaned heavily against the car.

"Be sure to cool him down. The wind is whipping up pretty good."

Joyce worked quickly. By the time she put the horse blanket on Bo, the breeze that had felt good earlier had turned into a sharp wind. Larry loaded Bo and put the tack away. Bob was already in the car, slumped down in the seat. No one suggested watching the rest of the show. Joyce gave Bo his carrot and a final pat. She climbed in the car as Larry started the ignition.

There was little conversation on the way home. Joyce was sure Bob had a fever.

Back at the stable, Larry quickly put everything away and settled Bo. "Let's keep him in tonight. I'll check him tomorrow."

Joyce agreed and turned to Bob. "I'm afraid the chocolate kind of melted in the car earlier." He smiled as she continued, "Is there anything we can do for you?"

"No, thanks. I need a good night's sleep. Good night."

It was only later that Joyce realized Bob had said nothing about another show or riding Bo again. She would wonder in the coming months if he somehow knew he might not sit in his saddle again.

Chapter Eleven

Larry checked Bo daily. The stable was between barn managers, so it was necessary to pitch in for the evening feeding. Jan came back home. Bob had been to the doctor again and was on another, new medication for infection of the mucous membrane system. No one took time to saddle a horse or talk about any more shows.

The summer term ended at the seminary. Joyce and Larry left for a summer holiday in the Colorado mountains with Christina and Steve. After a refreshing vacation, they drove across Kansas toward home. They talked about the coming school year they would both have and the horses they were eager to see again.

Larry mused, "I wonder how Sam is?"

"Who would have ever thought we'd have six horses? Will we take some of them back to The Back 40 this fall?"

"Probably the mares and Sam, now that he's weaned. I hope we can begin Magic's training soon."

"I want to ride Bo Jangles."

"Yes, you should try to ride him on a regular schedule now."

"I just hope everything is all right back at the stable."

Everything was not all right. Jan came hurrying out to the barn as she saw Joyce and Larry drive in.

"Hi, how was Colorado?"

"Great! Has everything been okay here?"

"The horses are fine. But Bob is much sicker. He's having a terrible time."

"Oh, no. Didn't the new medicine help?"

"No, in fact the doctor has continued to run tests and try different medications. They still don't really know what the matter is."

"Are there any new symptoms?"

"I'm afraid so. Besides the severe congestion, his face is swollen. There's swelling other places, and he has such aches and pains."

Larry put his arm around Jan. "I'm sorry. Surely the doctors will discover his problem soon. Joyce and I will handle all the problems in the barn."

Joyce agreed, "Oh, yes . . . and if there is anything else."

Feeding the six horses carrot treats she had brought was a bittersweet experience. But she was pleased Bo Jangles looked well and seemed happy to see her again.

"I did miss you so, and I bet the horse I rode in the mountains could never keep up with you."

Larry decided not to move the mares and Sam to The Back 40. "We'll keep them at the stable, because we may not have much time to go to the farm for a while."

Bob went to the hospital for more tests, including a bone-marrow test. Nothing was discovered. He returned home.

After a short visit, Joyce remarked to Larry, "Bob is so weak and looks like he's lost a lot of weight. And you know he was never overweight at all."

"I know. Bob finally told the dean to get a substitute for him at the seminary this quarter. Not knowing exactly what the problem is makes it impossible to plan ahead."

"Surely with a fall of complete rest he will begin to feel better."

"I wonder."

The next week Bob was back in the hospital. After a few days, he was moved to the large university hospital for more extensive tests.

Joyce went by the barn on Friday to do the evening feeding. Then she cleaned up to join Larry at the seminary for a retirement dinner. Larry greeted her at the door. She called to him. "Hi. Did I get all the hay out of my hair?"

"You look great. No one would ever know that thirty minutes ago you were mucking out. Everything okay there?"

"At the barn, yes. The filly wanted more attention than I had time for, but I got them all fed. No sign of Jan or anyone in the family. I wanted to ask about Bob."

"I just had a message to call the hospital later. Shall we go in to eat?"

Following the dinner, they went on to a party at a professor's home. After greeting everyone and talking over summer experiences, Larry looked at his watch and went into the bedroom to call the hospital. Joyce watched from the hall, while pretending to listen to the group's conversation. She saw Larry's shoulders sag and went to him. He slowly put the receiver down and looked at her. "It's acute leukemia."

Chapter Twelve

Bob came home three weeks later. He was on a weekend pass. Larry warned Joyce not to be shocked when she saw him.

After feeding the horses Saturday evening, they walked to the Carrigan's home. Bob was sitting on the porch, watching the pasture horses silhouetted by the sunset. He could not walk without help and was very weak. Yet he retained the good humor he'd always had.

The next day, Jan and their son helped Bob walk through the barn to where his stallions were stalled—three beautiful, spirited animals he'd tamed and ridden.

Back at the hospital the chemotherapy was increased. Every day brought a new complication. Another weekend pass ended before scheduled. Then he was moved to the Intensive Care Unit. Jan began living at the hospital. She and friends learned what **CODE BLUE** meant.

It was a rainy night as Larry pulled into the hospital parking garage. He and Joyce took the elevator to the third floor and found Jan. She left the ICU to have coffee with them.

Joyce asked, "Is there anything you need?"

"No."

"Are you eating regular meals?"

"Oh, most of the time. I do get out for a walk, and I drive home to check the mail most every day. My kids are great."

Joyce remarked that it must be a comfort having your grown children live in the same city.

"Yes, we take turns going in to see Bob. He can't talk with the respiratory tube in, but he gives us signals. He's so weak, but I don't think he's in much pain."

After tears and hugs, Joyce and Larry left to drive home. Jan's vigil continued.

One late-night trip was made to The Back 40 to winterize it. A pipe had already broken and flooded part of the house. Dejectedly, Larry surveyed the damage. "The floor is really soggy and we have no way to dry it out. I may have to replace this floor."

"But not tonight. Let's just leave it until spring. We have enough to think about." Joyce took his arm as he locked the door.

Then, one Friday night in mid-November, Joyce was finishing up in the boarding barn. Larry had gone over to the Carrigan's house to feed their dogs. The barn phone rang and Joyce answered. It was the hospital. Bob had died. Somehow it helped to stand and stroke Bo quietly. He didn't seem to mind the wet tears falling on his mane. "How do you say good-bye to a special friend—one you had shared an adventure with?"

The weekend was frantic, yet Jan continued to provide a calmness that was needed. Also, continuing with the regular schedule of living helped. Joyce was glad for the Saturday chores at home and the barn that kept her busy doing something.

On Sunday she sang in her church choir as usual. The anthem was, "If God Be for Us, Who Can Be Against Us?" That title phrase was sung over and over in a driving, pounding beat. Then the music changed to a quieter message, "For I am sure that neither death nor life, principalities, things present nor heights, nor anything else in all creation can separate us from the love of God in Christ Jesus our Lord." It was cathartic.

The memorial service for Bob was on Monday afternoon in the seminary chapel. The November day was overcast, with low-moving gray clouds. People hurried up the chapel steps to escape the ominous feel of the wind. By 3:00 P.M. the chapel was filled with family, friends, professional colleagues, students, and acquaintances from the Fox Trotter's Association. Jan had asked Larry to deliver the sermon.

After the chapel choir had sung and scriptures had been read, Larry stood up and walked to the pulpit. He'd found a scripture in the first chapter of Zechariah about horses among the myrtle trees. "They are those who the Lord has sent to range through the world. . . . The world is still and at peace." The people left the chapel to return to the world.

Chapter Thirteen

Mechanically Joyce lived through the remaining weeks of November and then December. Larry went by the stable after work each day. A new trainer was assuming management of the barn. Joyce went out often to help and see the six horses she missed so much. There never seemed to be time to ride in the indoor arena. The weather was too unpleasant outside.

Christmas week turned from an unpleasant cold to an unbearable − 20°. The barn pipes and pasture ponds froze. Every task was so much harder. Christina and Steve helped during the time they were home for the holidays.

January and February's weather was almost unrelenting. Weather records were broken every week. Still, the horses had to be cared for daily. March brought an ice storm that almost paralyzed the city for a week. Power lines fell and tore down fences at the stable. Larry repaired those and told Joyce later, "At least the electricity in the barn is on again."

"Do you think spring will ever come? I can't believe we will ever be able to ride our horses again. Oh, how I would like to be having spring at The Back 40!"

The frozen ground turned into mud, and the chores continued. Larry made plans to return the mares to the farm before they foaled. Little Sam had been sold.

The fields were sprouting green as the horse trailer turned in at The Back 40 gate. It was like returning to a world they had lived in a long time before. After being unloaded, the mares began to check out "home" again.

"I always wonder if they remember this place when they are brought back."

"I know; I do too." Larry watched the mares go to the familiar feed boxes in the barn. "I think they remember where the oats should be."

The pattern of going to The Back 40 for part of the weekends began again. The repairs to the house after the November flooding were not as extensive as Larry had first feared. It felt good to watch and experience the renewal of spring. The wild flowers seemed brighter than ever.

Carmen had a filly in May. Larry named her Secret Song. A month later Jennie's new filly, Golden Duchess, greeted them on a Sunday afternoon when they arrived from the city.

Joyce was delighted with the new little foal.

"She's elegant. And she's our first foal that didn't start out black. Look how she holds her head."

"Yes, she's the color of Bob's chestnut stallion, Carbon. Bob would have loved this one." They were silent, remembering.

Chapter Fourteen

Back at the stable in the city, Joyce took Bo out to ride on a sunny Saturday afternoon. It did not go well, and she was discouraged.

"I just can't get him to recall the gait. Of course he's not used to me in the saddle. I'm afraid I'm only confusing him."

Larry tried, without much more success. Finally he said, "I'm not doing much better, and I really don't have the time to ride him regularly."

"Let's take him to Luther. He helped train Bob's stallions."

Larry agreed and said, "We'll take the filly, too. I don't think we could part them anyway. Luther can start her training."

Joyce asked, "What about Magic?"

Larry thought a bit and then replied, "I want to keep working with him myself."

Larry delivered Bo Jangles and Joy to the trainer. It was hard for Joyce to stay away. After two and a half weeks, she persuaded Larry to go back with her for a visit. Anxiously, Joyce walked into the barn while Larry discussed the horses' progress with Luther. First she stopped to visit in the filly's stall, and then she went on to Bo Jangles.

"Oh, look at you all groomed up so special. Aren't you the handsome black horse?" She fed him carrot bits and rubbed him under his thick, straight mane.

Luther rode the two horses, showing off their trained gaits. They had done well in the short time under Luther's command. Joyce was pleased with the filly's progress after her first short time of training. But she was more eager to see Bo Jangles perform, and her eyes were more intent as she watched him step smartly around the ring, responding to Luther's touch. She remembered watching him a year ago in another ring with another rider. After the horses had been rubbed down and returned to their stalls, Luther asked, "Are you thinking of riding them in competition next year?"

Larry answered, "No, we really don't have the time or interest for that. It was a special time with Bob, but we want to take them to our farm in the woods for pleasure riding."

Joyce asked, "When do you think we could take them?"

Luther replied, as he closed the barn door, "Give them another week or so. That should get them ready for you to have a good ride."

Two weeks later, when Bo Jangles and Joy were unloaded at the farm and released from the lead ropes, they did not cautiously explore the fields as the mares had. Instead, they rolled and then ran with abandon. They were free again.

"He knows he is free again. I do so love to see him run and romp. This past year has been rough on him, too."

"Yes, but we don't want either of them to lose the discipline they've just had."

"I can't wait to ride him. He looks great."

At fifteen hands, Bo had nearly reached his full height. He had wide-set eyes in a short face with a prominent muzzle. His short back and straight legs resulted in a compact look. Larry said, "He looks much like his sire, the old Bo."

Magic was also returned to the farm for Larry to train him there. Gradually, the mares relaxed and accepted the colts and older filly to be around the barn and younger foals.

Larry cleared out an area by the barn for the impromptu riding ring. He took turns riding Magic and the filly, Joy. Joyce rode Bo Jangles. She would lead him to a stump or empty crate so she could mount. He would wait patiently until she was ready to move. Her arthritic arms and knees would no longer pull her up on their own.

After a month of riding around the circle Joyce asked,

"Can't we ride now in the field and not just around the ring? Bo and I are bored with that."

Larry agreed with her suggestion, and she took off across the pasture. It did appear Bo liked to stride out across a field or up a gentle slope much better.

"He's working well for you," Larry commented as he rode Magic up beside Joyce and Bo. "He's holding his head arched right, and he's a good size for you."

Joyce smiled. "Every ride gets better." As they rode, Joyce sang little ditties to Bo like she had when he was so young. His ears turned to the sound and kept the gait smooth. Joyce felt she could ride forever.

Bo began following Joyce around the farm again and would check her pockets out for a sugar or apple. At three years of age, he was at that adolescent stage of being childish one moment and then later being mature and responsible.

Joyce noted that he often stood guard over the new chestnut filly, Duchess, when Jennie wandered away from the sleeping foal to graze at a short distance.

"Oh, Bo, I bet you will be the one to comfort Duchess when she is weaned from her mama like you did Joy." Then, as he watched her intently, she continued, "I really think you know what I say to you."

There was no question of not communicating as they rode over the fields and up the bluffs. Bo's steady cadence rustled the leaves as they explored areas down by the big creek that flowed through the south border of The Back 40. Often a hawk would soar overhead as he guarded his wooded territory. Occasionally a deer would leap out of a hiding place and run off with his white tail flagging his route.

Then, in early October, Joyce had a serious physical relapse that interrupted her work and every other activity. There could be no horseback riding for six weeks.

Finally, one November Sunday afternoon, when the skies were the slate-gray of an overcast day, Joyce saddled Bo. Carefully, she mounted him as he stood patiently waiting. At her signal he began to move slowly and smoothly. She rode alone across a pasture to the bluffs overlooking the creek. A calm breeze stirred the leaves remaining on the trees. A flock of geese could be heard and then seen as the *V* in flight headed south.

They stopped at the top of the bluff. For a brief moment the sun shone through the treetops before losing its setting brilliance to the gray clouds. In the quiet, Joyce spoke in a soft voice heard only by Bo's alert ears.

"It's been a year, Bob. We miss you so much. I hope you know how well Bo Jangles is doing. He is winner for me. And, Bob, so were you."

The soaring hawk screeched warning as Joyce slowly turned Bo around and headed home in the smooth, steady fox-trot gait.